ORIL

JUNIOR SURVIVAL LIBRARY

Gentle giant in danger

THE ELEPHANT

Malcolm Penny

ANGLIA
Television Limited

Boxtree

Key to abbreviations

lb	pound
kg	kilogram
in	inch
ft	foot
yd	yard
cm	centimetre
m	metre
km	kilometre
sq mile	square mile
sq km	square kilometre
kph	kilometres per hour
mph	miles per hour

First published in 1990 by Boxtree Limited
Copyright © 1990 Survival Anglia Limited
Text copyright © 1990 Malcolm Penny

Front jacket photographs:
Survival Anglia/Jen & Des Bartlett
(Elephant scenting the air with its trunk
and Herd of African elephants)
Back jacket photograph:
Survival Anglia/Joanna Van Gruisen
(Asian elephant bathing)

Line drawings by Raymond Turvey

British Library Cataloguing in Publication Data
Penny, Malcolm
　The elephant.
　1. Elephants.
　I. Title II. Series
　599.61

ISBN 1-85283-057-3

Edited by Miranda Smith
Designed by Groom & Pickerill
Typeset by Rowland Phototypesetting Limited
Bury St Edmunds, Suffolk

Printed and bound in Italy
by OFSA s.p.a.

for Boxtree Limited,
36 Tavistock Street,
London WC2E 7PB

Contents

Elephants of the World 4

The First Elephants 6

Life in the Herd 8

Food and Water 10

Elephants on the Move 12

Senses and Signals 14

Poaching and the Ivory Trade 16

Too Many Elephants 18

The Captives 20

Elephants at Work 22

Elephants in History 24

Threats to the Elephants 26

Protecting Elephants 28

Glossary and Notes on Author 30

Index 31

Acknowledgements 32

Elephants of the world

An elephant must be one of the most extraordinary animals. With its huge bulky body, legs like pillars, large ears, and long flexible trunk, it looks like nothing else on Earth.

There are only two species of elephant in the world, African and Asian elephants. Both are about the same size, up to 3 m (9 ft) tall, and weighing as much as 5 tonnes.

The easy way to tell them apart in a zoo is that they have ears shaped like a map of the country which they come from. The African elephant has large rounded ears, and the Asian elephant has smaller ears which come to a point at the bottom, like the map of India. It is not necessary to know the difference between them in the wild, because they live so far apart. The African elephant now lives only in the southern part of Africa, and the Asian elephant in India and Sri Lanka, with a few in Sumatra and Malaysia.

There are still about 609,000 elephants in Africa. This might sound a lot, but between 1986 and 1989 over 300,000 were killed by poachers who took the tusks to sell for ivory.

Asian elephants are much less common.

An elephant's trunk

An elephant's trunk is a tube formed from its nose and top lip joined together. It is controlled by muscles and works like an arm with a hand on the end. It is a nose for sniffing the air, and a hosepipe for sucking up water. Asian elephants have a smooth trunk with one fingerlike shape on the end, and African elephants have a wrinkled trunk with two 'fingers'.

Asian elephants have small pointed ears.

Altogether there may be about 40,000 in the wild, and about 13,500 **domesticated** working animals. India has about 20,000 wild elephants. They are found in smaller numbers in eight other countries (see box on page 26), and in all of them they are classified as endangered in the **I.U.C.N. Red List** for 1988.

African elephants have large rounded ears, which look like the shape of Africa on the map.

In this book, we shall find out about the way elephants live, why they are all in some danger, and what can be done to save them.

The first elephants

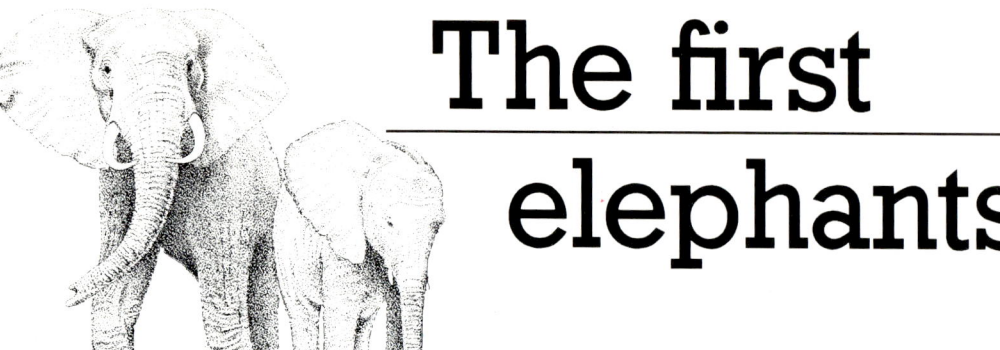

The oldest **fossil** elephants lived in North America about 45 million years ago. They had small tusks, but no trunk. They looked more like hippopotamuses, and lived in similar conditions.

About ten million years later, elephants with quite large tusks had **evolved**. They used the tusks for digging. By 20 million years ago elephants had a trunk. In the *Just So Stories*, by Rudyard Kipling, the elephant gets his trunk in a fight with a crocodile, who pulls his nose until it stretches, but this is meant to be a joke. In fact, trunks appeared over a very long period of time.

We shall never really know how elephants' trunks evolved, but by studying fossils scientists have worked out how it might have happened. As animals grow taller, they need to be able to reach the ground, to collect food and water. Giraffes evolved a long neck, but elephants of long ago developed long jaws and lips instead. When the jaws became shorter,

A manatee's snout looks like an elephant's trunk.

The rock hyrax is a distant relative of elephants.

the top lip and the nose remained as a trunk.

Ten million years ago, there were many species of elephants living all over the world. Now most have died out, though at least one other species survived until the first humans appeared on Earth. In caves where Stone Age people lived, there are drawings of woolly mammoths. These were elephants of the northern hemisphere with woolly coats and curved tusks over 3 m (9 ft) long. Their bodies have been found frozen into glaciers, and in the **permafrost** of Siberia and Alaska. Now there are just two species of elephant left.

Relatives of elephants

Scientists studying evolution have discovered that there are two types of animal living today which came from the same ancient family as the elephants. One is the manatee, or sea cow, which lives in tropical oceans. The other is the hyrax, a small furry animal which lives in rocky places in Africa. Fifty million years ago, when the first elephants were beginning to appear, both manatees and hyraxes were very similar to them, though they went on to evolve in very different ways!

Life in the herd

Elephants live in **social** groups called herds, which are composed of members of one or more families. The herd travels from one waterhole or feeding place to another, along paths which may have been used for centuries.

A group of adult bulls leads the way, followed by groups of cows, walking close together, with the young ones in the middle, in case of danger. At the back of the herd there are usually a few more bulls, with any elephants which have been injured.

The herd works together to help all its members. When a new baby is born, all the other adults form a ring round the mother, and one or two of the older females act as 'midwives', helping the mother, and lifting the baby for its first steps. The baby is about 1 m (3 ft) tall, and weighs 1 kg (2 lbs) when born.

When the herd moves on, one of the older females will help the mother to support her youngster, and within a few days the other young elephants in the herd will be leading it about and playing with it.

Large bull elephants usually drive other adults away from their feeding places, until they have finished eating. However, they always make room for a youngster, sometimes even collecting and cleaning grass for it, or breaking up branches into small pieces which the baby can manage.

In this peaceful and co-operative way, a herd of wild elephants wanders far and wide, in search of the enormous quantities of food and water which it needs to keep it going.

Elephants and eland at a waterhole in Namibia.

Above *Baby elephants are treated very gently by adults.*

Below *The dust flies as elephants powder themselves after a bath.*

Water and dust

Elephants take great care of their skin. Although the skin is 2–4 cm (1–1½ in) thick, it is very sensitive, and needs regular washing. After wallowing in a muddy pool, the elephants dry themselves by powdering their skin with dust, which they pick up in their trunks and blow over their backs.

Food and water

A fully-grown adult elephant can eat 300 kg (660 lbs) of green food each day. Although they eat roots, bark, and even wood, they prefer sweet grasses and bamboo shoots, and especially fig leaves.

To reach as high as they can, elephants stand up on their hind legs and raise their trunk to pull down the branches of a tree. They will sometimes knock small trees down so that they can eat the leaves at the top.

All elephants need between 70 and 90 litres (120–150 pints) of water every day. They suck it up in their trunk, and squirt it into their mouth, about 8 litres (14 pints) at a time.

During the dry season, elephants use their tusks, trunk and feet to dig for water, sometimes making a hole several metres deep. This helps other animals as well, since they can use the hole after the elephants have gone. If conditions become too dry, the elephants might move on to another place. When that happens, many other animals will die, without the elephants to help them to find water.

When food is very scarce, elephants often strip the bark from trees in search of the last scrap of nourishment. This kills the trees, and the elephants are in danger of destroying their own food supply.

Opposite *Holes dug by elephants are useful to other animals later.*

An elephant's trunk is useful for reaching after food.

Elephants on the move

Asian elephants move through the forests along paths which may have been used for a hundred years. These elephant 'roads' are also used by many other animals. In Africa, where the elephants live in much more open country, they still follow a regular circuit from one watering or feeding place to another.

Before people occupied so much of the land in India and Africa, a herd of elephants could roam freely over a large area. When the food in one place had been used up, they could move on to another. By the time their wanderings brought them back to the first place, the vegetation would have grown up once more, so that they had a new supply of food.

As the numbers of people increased, they drove the elephants away, or even killed them, to stop them trampling and eating their crops. There was less and less room for the elephants to continue their wandering way of life.

Today, most elephants are fenced in, inside parks and reserves. There may be just enough land in a park to support the elephants which live there, but there is no room for any increase in the elephant population.

In Tsavo National Park, in Kenya, the elephants multiplied to such an extent that in a **drought** in 1960 they completely destroyed the food supply for themselves and other

Left *This baby elephant died of thirst.*

animals, and very many animals died. In countries where elephants are still numerous, their numbers have to be controlled to protect the parks. Sadly, this means that some of them have to be shot, or **culled**.

Above *An elephant can charge at speed of up to 40 kph.*

Below *Elephants march in single file from one waterhole to the next.*

Senses and signals

Elephants do not need to see very well because they are forest animals, and in the forest nobody can see very far because of the thick vegetation. They signal to each other by moving their ears, raising them when they are uneasy, and folding them flat when they are about to charge. Much more important, however, are their senses of smell and hearing.

They have a very good sense of smell, which they use when they sniff the air for signs of danger, as well as to recognise each other. When two elephants meet, they touch each other's faces, to sniff the scent produced by **glands** which open on the temples and cheeks.

Eleanor, an orphan of the drought in Tsavo, uses her trunk to examine a jeep.

They often touch each other's mouths as well.

Elephants' hearing is also good. They make a variety of sounds to **communicate** with each other. Loud trumpeting noises are for communicating at a distance, or when they are frightened. Quieter sounds, like deep rumblings or soft piping calls, are made between friends, or from a mother to her baby. They can also communicate at a distance by making very deep noises which travel through the ground, so that other elephants can feel them through the soft soles of their feet.

The sense of touch is very important to an elephant. Some of their greeting movements may be touching as well as sniffing, and they use their trunks to feel the ground in front when they are walking. Strangely, they also use their sensitive trunks for signalling, by banging them on the ground when they are angry or unhappy. It sounds like somebody bouncing a car tyre.

The elephants' graveyard

There is an old story that when elephants realise that they are about to die, they go to a special place, to lie among the bones of their ancestors. This is not true. Where collections of elephant bones have been found, it is most likely that they are the result of a whole herd dying in one place during a bad drought.

Opposite *Elephants are curious about the bones of other elephants which have died.*

14

Poaching and the ivory trade

Ivory has been valuable for a very long time, because it is a beautiful smooth, creamy-white material, and very good for carving. For people to have ivory, elephants must be killed, so that their tusks can be sawn off. The trade in ivory is now so great that **poachers** kill as many as 70,000 elephants in Africa every year. In several African countries like Kenya, Uganda and Somalia, there are hardly any elephants left. Asian elephants are not hunted so much, since they have only small tusks, and a number of them have no tusks at all.

It is now illegal to import ivory into the United States and the European Community, after Tanzania asked for the trade to be banned in the hope of saving some of its last surviving elephants. Ivory became less valuable when the ban was announced, because fewer people would be able to buy it legally. Soon, it might be illegal to trade in ivory anywhere in the world.

However, the trade still continues through Hong Kong, Singapore, Taiwan and Japan, and ivory is smuggled all over the world.

Some ancient ivory carvings, made by great artists, especially in China, Japan and India, are very beautiful. The modern imitations are nothing like as good. It might seem sad that the art of ivory carving should die out, but it would be sadder still if elephants were to die out only to supply the market with cheap mass-produced souvenirs.

Some countries such as Zimbabwe, Botswana and South Africa do not want a complete ban on the ivory trade. They have to cull some of their elephants every year to protect their parks. They would like to continue to sell the valuable ivory and use the money to keep their parks going.

Left *Poachers kill many thousands of elephants every year for the ivory trade.*

Opposite *In Zimbabwe, elephants in some National Parks must be culled to reduce their number.*

Too many elephants?

In some places in Africa, there are too many elephants. In Hwange National Park, in Zimbabwe, the park rangers have to cull 200 elephants every year to keep the herds the right size. The rangers want to avoid the disaster which hit Tsavo in 1960.

Elephants breed very readily in good conditions. A female can bear her first calf when she is about ten years old. The **gestation period** is 22 months, and the female can produce young for about 27 years. In her lifetime, she might have seven or eight calves.

A group of 2,000 elephants produces 200 calves every year – a population of elephants can grow very quickly. In an enclosed park,

Airlift. A young elephant is transported by air to a new home in a protected area.

which is where most elephants live, they can soon outgrow the space available to them. If the park is not enclosed, any 'spare' elephants will wander outside, and soon be in trouble from farmers.

There was a time when spare elephants could be moved to other parks which needed new stock, or to zoos. Some of the young ones from culled herds are still sent to zoos, but there is nowhere for the adults to go. They are slow to settle down in unfamiliar country, among strange elephants, and if they were sent to parks in countries to the north of Zimbabwe, they would be shot by poachers as soon as they arrived.

It is a very difficult problem. The value of the ivory from culled elephants would be enough to finance Zimbabwe's parks for many years, but if it were to be sold it would only encourage the market for ivory, and give the poachers a reason to continue poaching.

Uganda once had huge herds of elephants. This one lives in a national park.

The captives

Until very recently, Asian elephants in India were captured in the wild and trained to work for people, as they have been for over 5,000 years.

The traditional way of catching elephants was to drive them across country, with men on other, trained, elephants, until they were trapped in a stockade. Then the catchers rode into the stockade on their trained elephants, and tied up the captives before leading them away, each roped between two tame elephants.

To train the new elephants, the men would keep them awake for two or three nights, lighting fires round them, and singing to them. The elephants were forced to go without food until they were so tired and hungry that they would put up with the men touching them, and eventually riding on their backs.

The youngest elephants were kept with their mothers, to be trained later when they had grown up a little. Young elephants are not strong enough to work, and very difficult to train, so it is left until they are ten years old.

The captives settled down very quickly,

Captive wild elephants in a stockade are lassoed.

An elephant and her baby enjoy a bath from their trainer.

making friends with the other tame elephants, and soon learning the words of command. Within six months they would be working in the forest.

Now there are so few wild elephants left that the Indian government has banned any further captures. Instead, they will have to be bred in captivity and trained to work in the forests and in ceremonial processions.

Scientific capture

When elephants have to be moved from one place to another, scientists use drugs to put them to sleep. The drugs are usually given to the elephant by injection with a syringe fired from a gun, often from a helicopter. When the elephant has been carried to its new home, another injection counteracts the effect of the drug, and the animal wakes up again.

Trainers keeping newly-captured elephants awake with fire and singing.

21

Elephants at work

Trained elephants still work in the forests of India. They are much better than machines at carrying loads over steep and awkward ground. They can lift logs weighing 2 tonnes, and put them where they are told, like intelligent four-legged bulldozers. By the age of 20, a fully-trained elephant understands and obeys 27 different words of command.

Because their 'fuel' grows on trees, elephants are also cheaper to run than bulldozers. They do not burn **fossil fuels**, so they do not pollute the air. Using them for forestry work is better than machines for another reason. The floor of a forest is made of very **fragile** soil, which is easily compressed by heavy vehicles. This makes it unsuitable for planting new trees or crops. Although elephants are very heavy, they have enormous feet, so that their weight is spread over a large area. This means that they do much less damage to the forest floor than machines.

For thousands of years, trained elephants have been used to carry people. Elephants are still used for special processions, often painted and dressed in beautiful costumes.

In the National Parks of Nepal and India, rangers use elephants as they go about their work, and visitors can ride them when they go out to see tigers and rhinoceroses.

A trained elephant can lift heavy logs, and put them down where it is told.

Opposite *Beautifully painted, a ceremonial elephant leads a parade in Sri Lanka.*

Training African elephants

The African elephant is not used as a work animal in the same way as the Asian, although some animals from the north of the country, where they are now extinct, were trained in ancient times. There is one small experimental training school for African elephants in Zaire, where it has been proved that they can be trained, but they cannot work as hard or for as long as Asian elephants.

Elephants in history

The most famous elephants in European history must be those which the young Carthaginian general Hannibal used to cross the Alps in 218 BC. The use of elephants was very successful in battle against the Romans, because their size frightened the enemy soldiers, and the enemy horses were terrified by their smell.

The Carthaginians and other Mediterranean peoples used to catch and train the small North African race of elephants known as Atlas elephants. Since they did not trouble to breed them in captivity, but simply went out to catch some more when they needed them, the elephants became extinct.

Above *A carved elephant on the wall of a temple in Kandy, Sri Lanka.*

Elephant racing was a favourite sport of the old emperors of India.

There is evidence that Asian elephants were trained in India as early as 3500 BC. Their pictures were used on coins and carved into the walls of temples from that day to this. The great Mogul emperors used elephants not only in battles and processions, but also for racing and fighting. One of the Hindu gods is an elephant, called Ganesha, who is worshipped as the god of wisdom and foresight.

Although trained elephants become very friendly with their *mahouts*, or drivers, they are not really domestic animals, because they have not so far been bred in captivity. Now that they are no longer caught in the wild, this will have to change.

The elephants often seem as excited as their mahouts.

Polo on elephant-back

At Tiger Tops, a tourist centre in the Royal Chitwan National Park in Nepal, elephants are used every day to carry visitors through the grass jungle to see the animals. Once a year there is a polo match between two teams mounted on elephants. This is done mostly for fun, but it raises money for charity as well.

Threats to the elephant

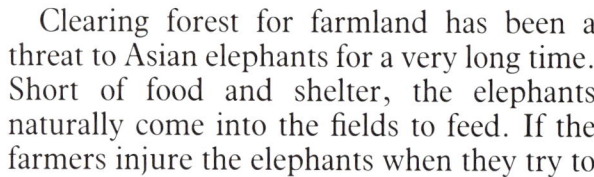

There are two main threats to the survival of elephants: wherever they live they are in danger from the loss of their forest **habitat**, and in Africa they are also at risk from poachers who kill them for the ivory trade.

Clearing forest for farmland has been a threat to Asian elephants for a very long time. Short of food and shelter, the elephants naturally come into the fields to feed. If the farmers injure the elephants when they try to

Where the elephants are

Africa (all countries)*	625,000
India	22,300
Bangladesh	250
Sri Lanka	2,500
Nepal	45
Burma	5,000
Thailand	3,000
Indonesia	3,000
Sabah	1,000
Malaysia	800
China	230

*There are 36 African countries that have some elephants, but only five of them have stable or increasing elephant populations. The five are Zimbabwe, Malawi, South Africa, Botswana and Namibia.

A baobab tree which has been wrecked by hungry elephants.

An elephant herd takes an evening drink at the waterhole.

drive them away, the elephants can become angry, and this often results in injuries and deaths, both human and animal.

As the human population grew, the danger to the elephants increased. But the worst danger came in the late 1800s when British people went to India to grow tea in huge plantations. To protect the plantations, many elephants were captured or shot, along with the rhinoceroses and tigers which also lived in the forests. This went on in the other countries where the Asian elephants live, until now there are only about 40,000 left in the world.

African elephants, too, have been pushed aside by **cultivation**. They have also destroyed parts of their own habitat where they have been shut into reserves and parks without enough space to follow their normal wandering way of life.

Ivory poachers used to catch elephants with **snares**, or by digging deep pits, covered with sticks and grass, so that the elephants would fall in. Nowadays, they shoot them with powerful automatic rifles. Between 1986 and 1989, they killed a total of 300,000 elephants. Unless the slaughter stops, there will soon be no African elephants left in the wild.

Protecting elephants

The only way to stop poaching is to stop the ivory market. If no one in the world wanted to buy ivory, the traders would not pay the poachers for it, and so they would stop hunting. Until this happens, all African elephants will be in danger.

Protecting the Asian elephants' forest habitat means thinking how to share the land with elephants. Crop-growers and elephants could then live side by side. This can be achieved by making sure that whenever land is cleared for planting, wide strips of trees are left untouched, so joining the remaining forest patches together. These 'green corridors' can then be used by the animals to move from one patch of forest to another.

In Malaysia, where the oil palm is a valuable crop, elephant damage has cost the planters a great deal of money. To protect their crops, the planters use electric fences which startle the elephants without harming them. Other countries are beginning to try the same thing.

In Thailand, the World Wide Fund for Nature is helping to protect elephants by teaching the local people how to grow better crops on the land they have already, so that they need not clear any more forest.

Protecting elephants is necessary so that people can come from far away to admire them, and this can help by bringing money to poor countries. However, this is not all – it is also vital for the survival of these gentle giants.

African elephants at home with some impala.

Opposite *Asian elephants need forests to survive.*

Glossary

Communicate Exchange messages.

Culled Killed to keep the herds the right size.

Cultivation Using land to grow crops.

Domesticated Trained to work for humans.

Drought A long period without rain.

Evolved The slow process by which animals change over millions of years.

Fossil The remains of an ancient animal which have been preserved and turned to rock.

Fossil fuel Fuel such as coal, oil, or gas which is made from the remains of ancient plants and animals.

Fragile Easily damaged.

Gestation period The time between mating and producing a baby.

Gland An organ of the body which produces scent and other substances.

Habitat The place which is most suitable for an animal's home.

I.U.C.N. Red List A list of endangered animals prepared by the International Union for the Conservation of Nature and Natural Resources.

Permafrost Ground in polar regions which is frozen all the year round.

Poacher Someone who kills animals illegally for his own profit.

Snare A loop of wire which pulls tight to trap any animal which steps in it or puts its head through it.

Social Living together in groups.

About the author

Malcolm Penny has a B.Sc. Hons degree in zoology from Bristol University and led the Bristol Seychelles Expedition in 1964. He was also a member of the Royal Society Expedition to Aldabra in 1966. Malcolm has worked for the Wildfowl Trust and was the First Scientific Administrator I.C.B.P. on Cousin Island in the Seychelles. He now works as a producer of natural history programmes for Survival Anglia.

Index

The entries in **bold** are illustrations.

breeding 18
bathing 8, **8**, 21

calves 8, **8**, **12**, 18
ceremonies 21, 22, **23**, 25
charging **13**
culling 13, 16, **17**, 18, 19, 30

deer 12

ears 4, 14
elephant racing **25**
elephants
    African 4, **4**, 16, 22, 27, 28, **28**
    Asian 4, 5, 12, 16, 20, 22, 25, 26, 27, 28, **29**
    as midwives 8
    Atlas 24
    catching 20, **20**
    drugging 21
    in battle 25
    in the wild 5, **20**, 21
    'roads' 12
    working 20, 22–3, **22**
elephants' graveyard 14
eyes 14

feeding places 8, 10, 11, 12, 26, **26**
feet 10, 22

fossils 6, 30

Ganesha, the elephant god 25
giraffes 6

habitat 26, 28, 30
Hannibal 24
herds 8, **19**
hyraxes 7, **7**

I.U.C.N. Red List 5, 30
ivory 4, 16, 19, 27, 28
ivory carvings 16

jaws 6

Kipling, Rudyard 6
    Just So Stories 6

legs 4
lips 6

manatee **6**, 7
mahouts **24**, 25

park rangers 18, 22
parks 12, 13, **16**, 19, 22, 27
    Etosha National, Namibia **12**
    Hwange National, Zimbabwe 18

India National 22
    Royal Chitwan National, Nepal 22, 25
    Tsavo National, Kenya 12, **14**, 18
permafrost 7, 30
poachers 4, 16, **16**, 19, 26, 27, 28, 30
polo matches 25

rhinoceroses 12, 27

size 4, 8, 24
skin 8
smell 14
snares 27, 30
Stone Age caves 7

tigers 12, 27
training 22, 24
training schools 22
trunks 4, 6, 10, 11, 14
tusks 4, 6, 7, 10

waterholes 8, **13**
weight 4, 8
woolly mammoths 7
World Wide Fund for Nature 28

zoos 4, 19

Picture Acknowledgements

The publishers would like to thank the
Survival Anglia picture library
and the following photographers for the use
of photographs on the pages listed:

Bruce Davidson 5, 14, 16, 27; Dieter & Mary Plage 4, 15, 20, 21, 22, 23, 24, 25, 28; Jeff Foott 6; Bob Campbell 7, 26; Jen & Des Bartlett 8, 9, 12, 13; Alan Root 9, 18, 19; Cindy Buxton 11; Joan Root 10; Lee Lyon 13, 18; Ronald Watts 17; Joanna Van Gruisen 29.